AF575367

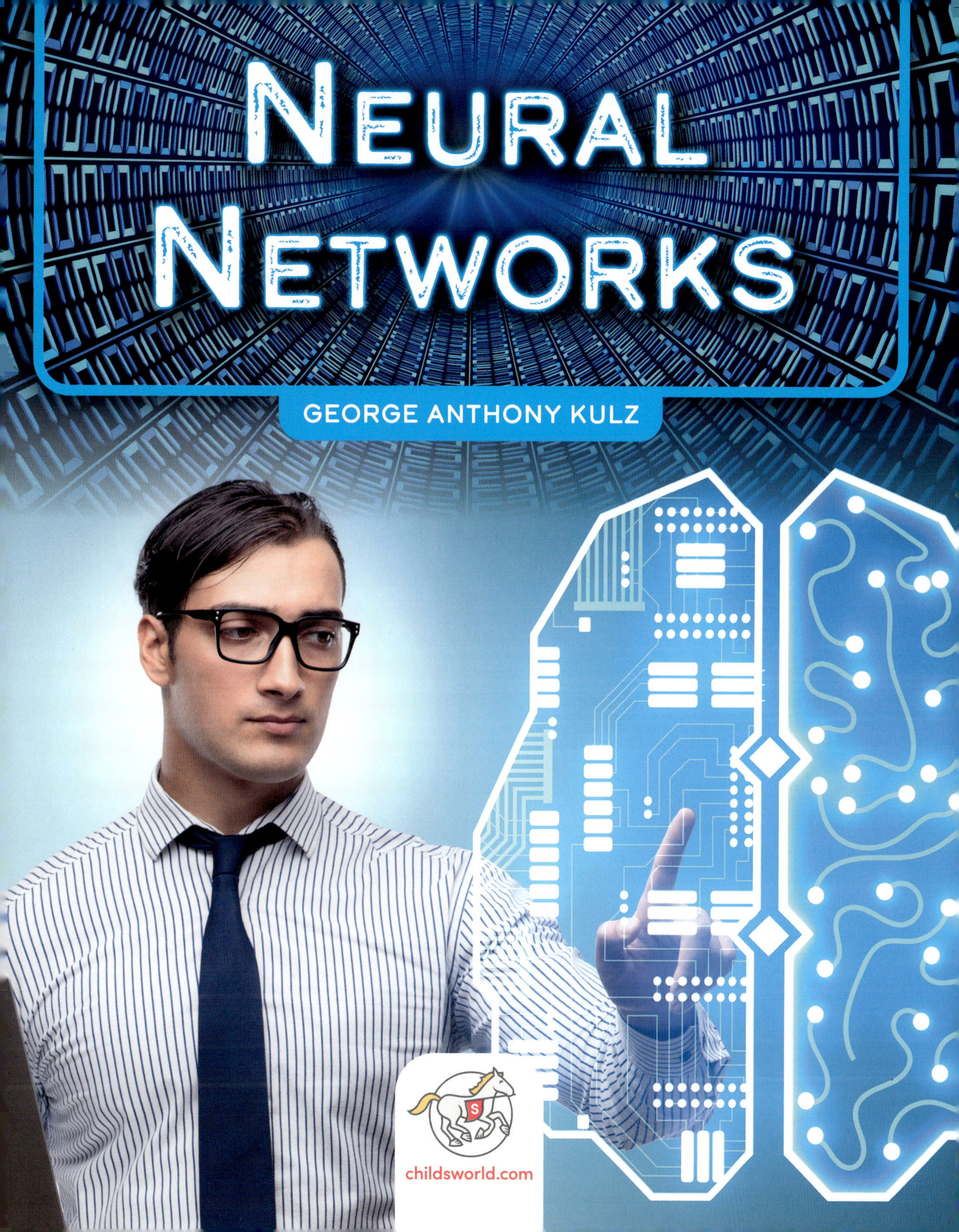
NEURAL NETWORKS
GEORGE ANTHONY KULZ
childsworld.com

Published by The Child's World®
800-599-READ • www.childsworld.com

Copyright © 2025 by The Child's World®
All rights reserved. No part of this book may be reproduced or utilized in any form or by any means without written permission from the publisher.

Photography Credits
Photographs ©: Shutterstock Images, cover, 1, 6, 11 (bottom), 12, 19, 20; Uli Deck/picture-alliance/dpa/AP Images, 5; Chalie Chulapornsiri/Shutterstock Images, 9; Oleksandr Drypsiak/Shutterstock Images, 11 (top); Roman Zaiets/Shutterstock Images, 13; Frederic Lewis/Archive Photos/Getty Images, 15; Panuwat Phimpha/Shutterstock Images, 16; Design elements from Tatiana Shepeleva/Shutterstock Images and Shutterstock Images

ISBN Information
9781503893832 (Reinforced Library Binding)
9781503894655 (Portable Document Format)
9781503895478 (Online Multi-user eBook)
9781503896291 (Electronic Publication)

LCCN 2024941407

Printed in the United States of America

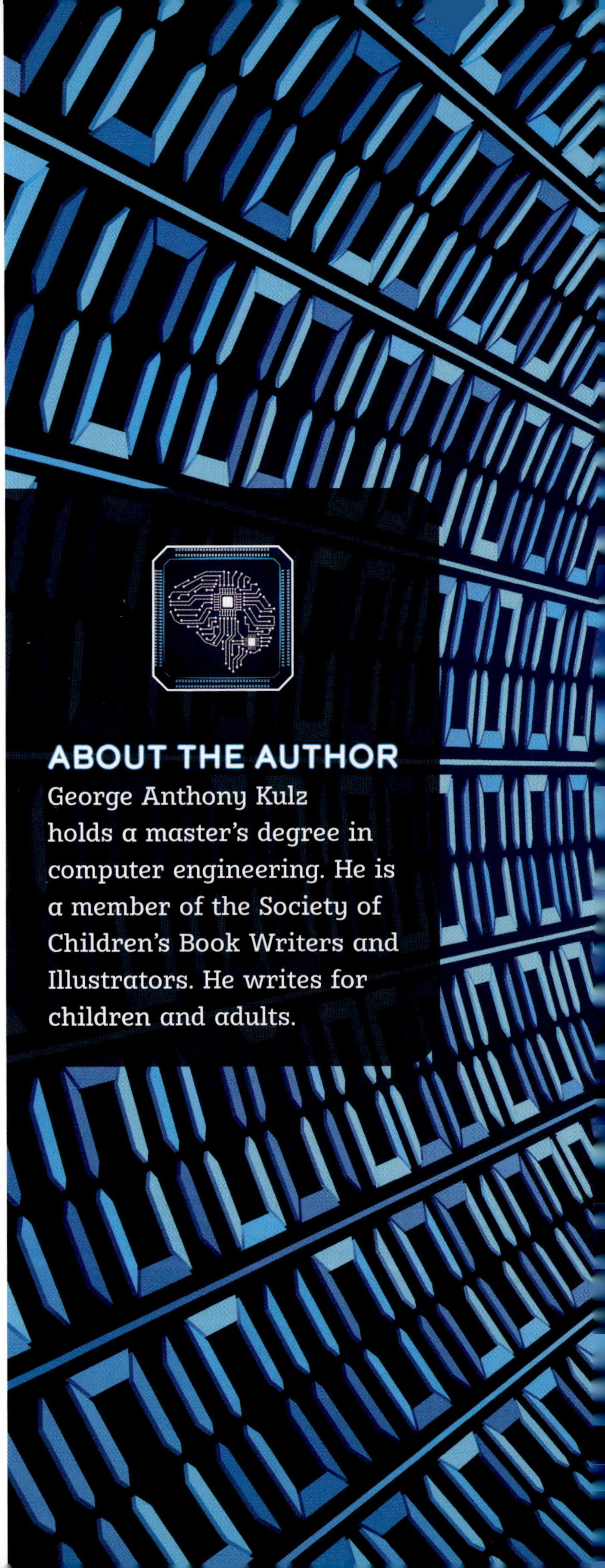

ABOUT THE AUTHOR

George Anthony Kulz holds a master's degree in computer engineering. He is a member of the Society of Children's Book Writers and Illustrators. He writes for children and adults.

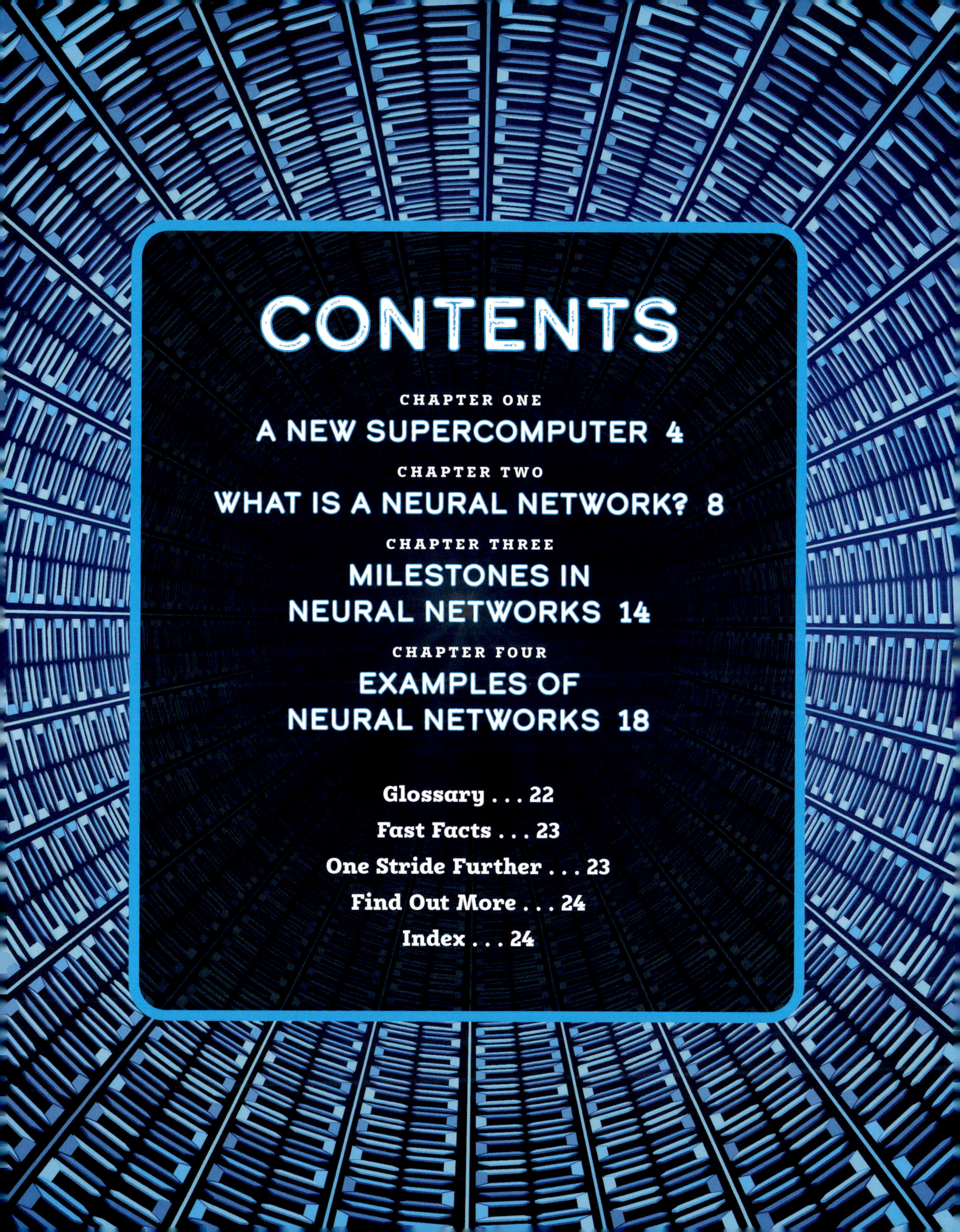

CONTENTS

CHAPTER ONE

A NEW SUPERCOMPUTER

In a university in Penrith, Australia, researchers were working on a special computer. It was called DeepSouth. DeepSouth was not an ordinary computer. It was a neuromorphic (nur-oh-MOR-fik) computer. Its design was inspired by the human brain. Researchers expected DeepSouth to be able to run 228 trillion instructions per second. This is around the same speed that the human brain can **process** information.

DeepSouth uses a neural network. A neural network is a kind of **program**. It is modeled after the human brain. Neural networks allow a computer to learn in a way that resembles how people learn. This is called machine learning. Neural networks are a kind of artificial intelligence (AI). AI is the ability of computers to do things that normally require human intelligence.

DeepSouth is an example of a supercomputer. These are special computers that are much more powerful than most other computers. The Karlsruhe high-performance computer (pictured) is located in Germany.

Neuromorphic computers are specially designed to work with neural networks. But people can use neural networks on regular computers as well.

Scientists hope to use DeepSouth to learn more about the brain. It may be used to study diseases such as Alzheimer's and Parkinson's. These diseases affect the brain. DeepSouth could also show how medicine affects the brain. It might also help people understand how the brain ages.

DeepSouth could also serve as an example for future computers. Computers today are limited. **Processors** can only be made so small. Too many small parts next to each other get too hot. But neuromorphic computers are designed differently than regular computers. This means that these computers may one day avoid the overheating issues of regular computers.

Neural networks are being used to solve real-world problems. They are used in many everyday devices, from cars to smartphones. In the future, neural networks could change much more. Medicine, entertainment, and weather prediction are only some of the fields that will benefit from this type of AI.

NEURAL NETWORKS AND SMARTPHONES

People use neural networks all the time. Modern image and voice recognition rely on them. These features are available on many smartphones. Image recognition allows people to unlock their phones with a face scan. Voice recognition allows people to give spoken commands to their phones.

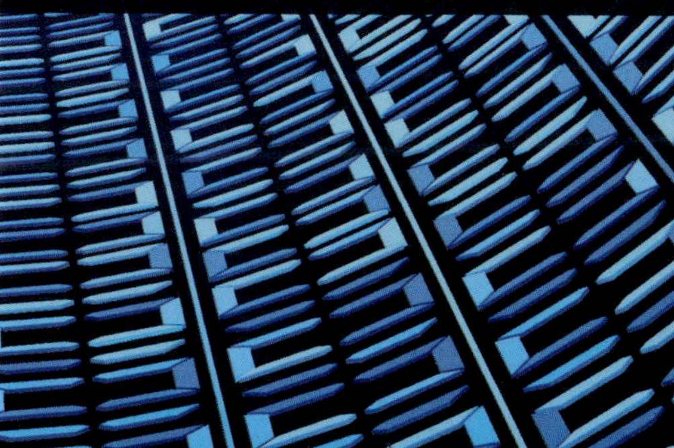

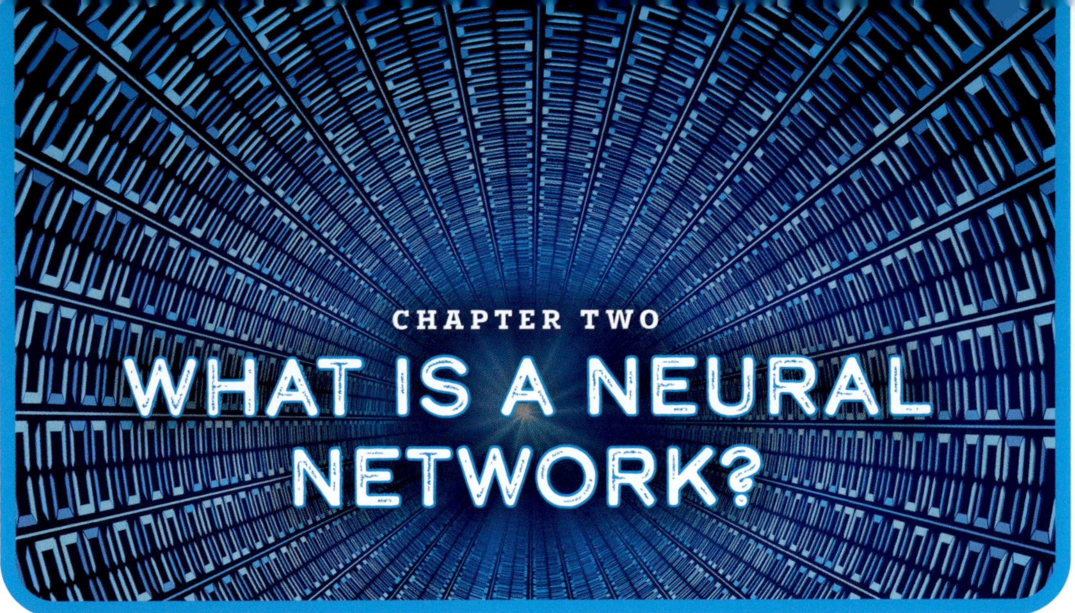

CHAPTER TWO

WHAT IS A NEURAL NETWORK?

Neural networks are broadly modeled after the human brain. The brain is made of cells. These cells are called neurons. Neurons pass signals among each other and to the rest of the body. A neuron has three main parts. Dendrites receive input signals from other cells. Dendrites look like the branches of a tree. The soma is the main part of the cell. It provides the energy the cell needs. The third part is called the axon. It sends output signals to other cells.

A neural network is a **structure** made of nodes. These nodes are also called perceptrons. A node is similar to a neuron. A node receives inputs from other nodes. The node processes the inputs to create an output. The node then sends the output to other nodes.

Doctors use MRI scans to check people's brains for problems.

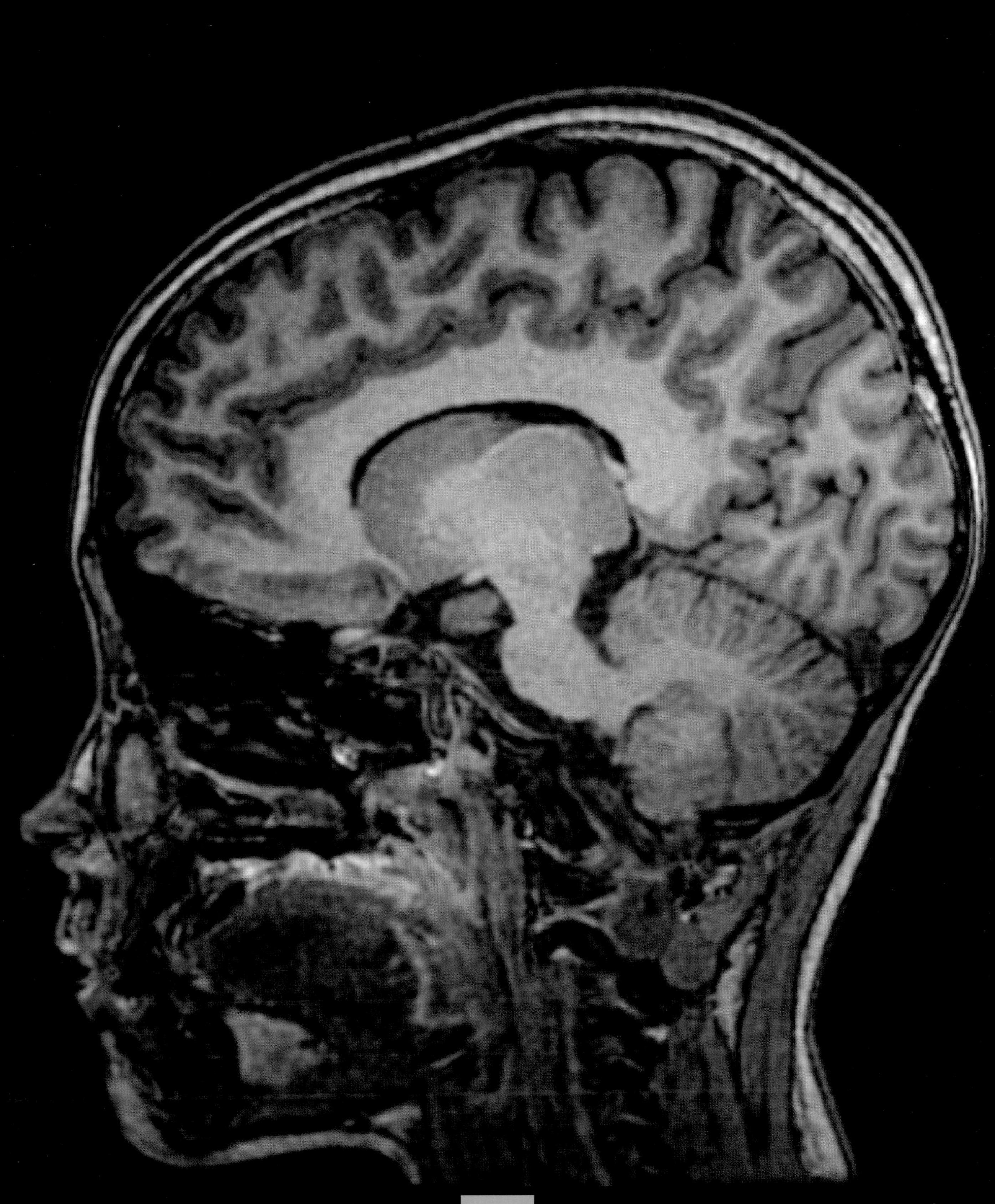

Neural networks learn by placing mathematical weights on each of the inputs of a node. This helps the network decide which information is most important. The higher the weight, the more important the information.

A node in a neural network is not exactly the same as a neuron. Neurons work with **electrical** and **chemical** signals. These signals are sent from one cell to another. A node in a neural network works with numbers. These numbers are sent from one node to another.

Like neurons in the brain, each node connects to many other nodes. Groups of nodes in a neural network are called layers. Each layer processes the **data** further. The last layer is called the output layer. It produces the neural network's final output.

Neural networks learn by processing lots of data over time. This allows neural networks to solve problems that are hard for other types of programs to solve. For example, a neural network can learn to recognize faces in images by looking at lots of pictures of people.

NEURONS AND NODES

Neuron in a Brain

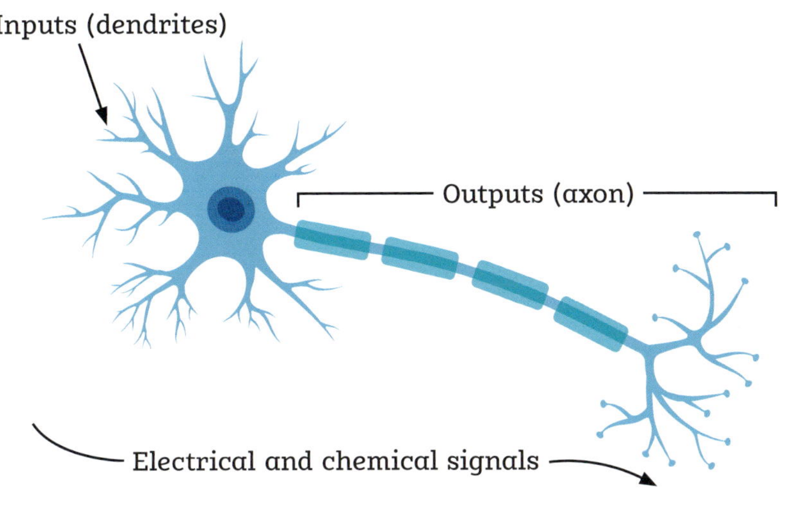

Nodes in a Neural Network

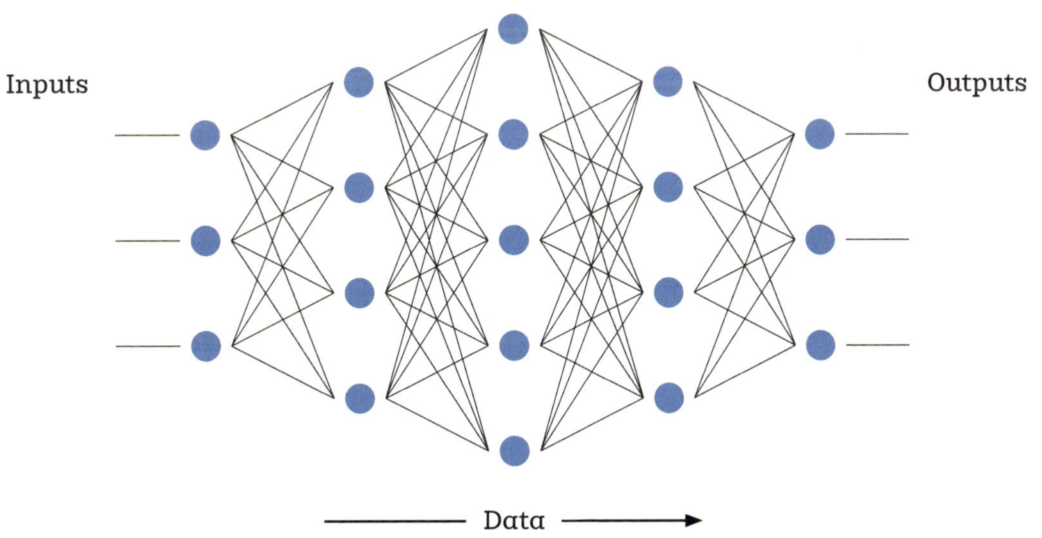

One major difference between neurons and nodes in a neural network is that neurons exist physically, while nodes can be mathematically modeled by computers.

Sometimes neural networks are given data from data centers. These are places full of computers that store data. Companies can pay to use this data.

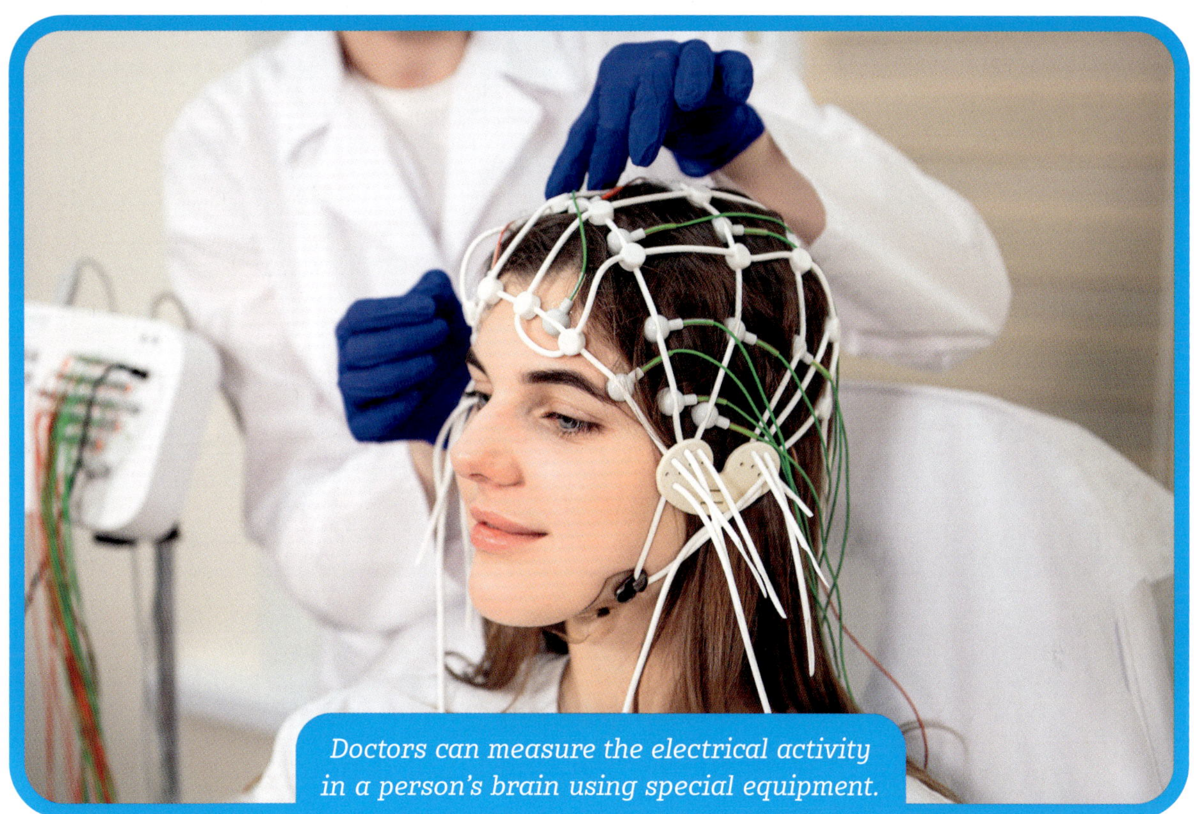
Doctors can measure the electrical activity in a person's brain using special equipment.

Deep-learning networks are a kind of neural network. They have three or more layers. Having multiple layers can allow a network to solve more complex problems.

Neural networks process a very large amount of data. Different types of neural networks learn from data in different ways. Some need people to mark data with labels. This helps the network find patterns in the data. For example, data consisting of images might be labeled based on what is in the images. An image might be labeled *tree* if it contains a tree. Other networks can find patterns in data on their own.

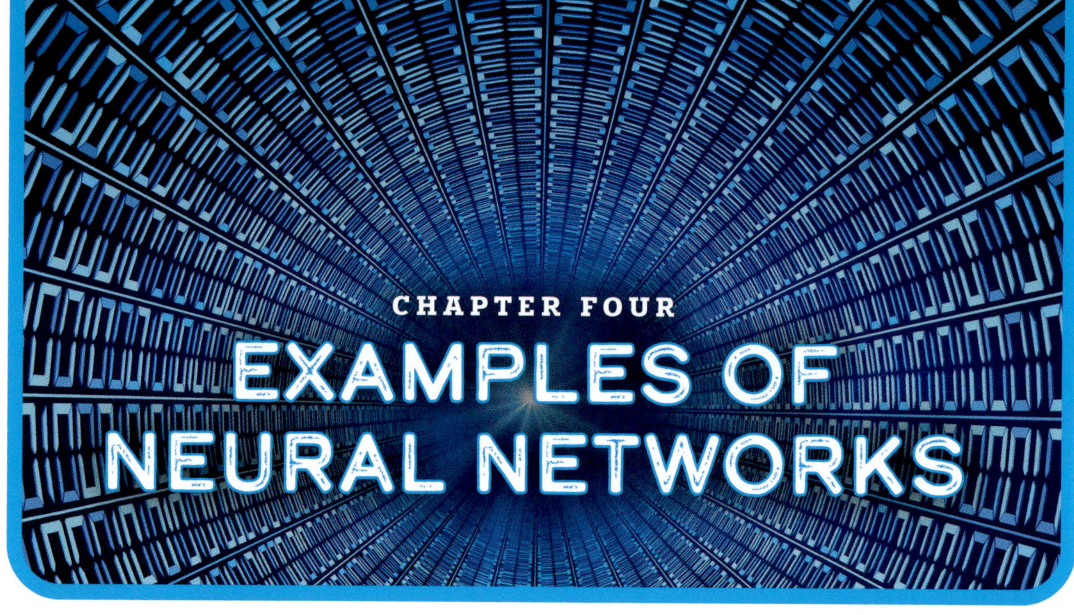

CHAPTER FOUR

EXAMPLES OF NEURAL NETWORKS

Today, neural networks are part of everyday life. Two popular examples of neural networks are ChatGPT and DALL-E. The company OpenAI developed them in the 2020s. They are examples of generative AI. Generative AI can create something new based on data it has learned. ChatGPT is a **chatbot** that can create humanlike text. It can also remember conversations. DALL-E can create images based on text descriptions that are given to it.

Stable Diffusion is another neural network that can create images. Like DALL-E, Stable Diffusion can create images based on text prompts. For example, a user can ask for a picture of a house. Stable Diffusion will create an image of a house based on the data on which it was trained.

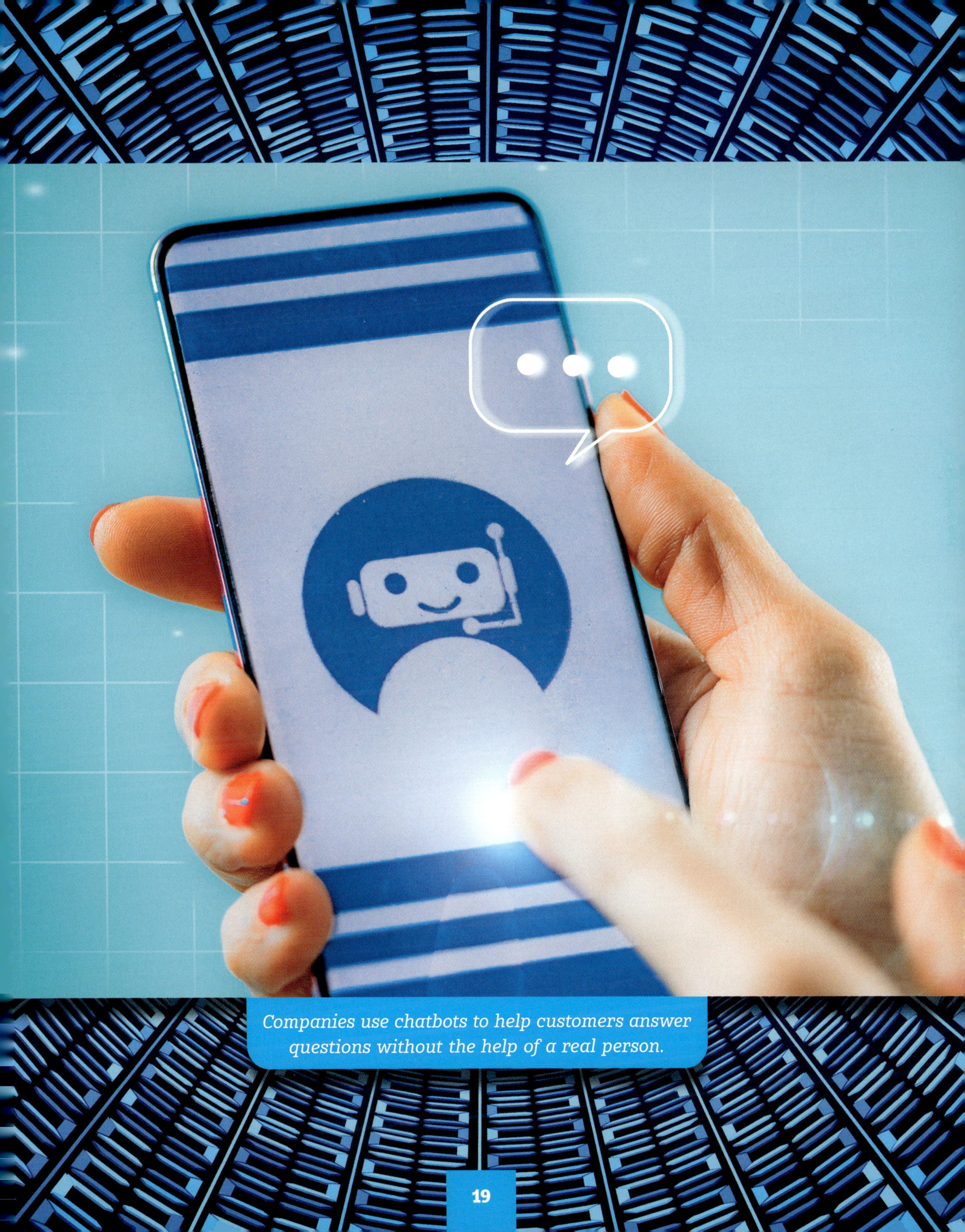

Companies use chatbots to help customers answer questions without the help of a real person.

AI assistants can be used in people's homes to do things such as turn on lights and play music on speakers.

Other examples of neural networks are recommender systems. Recommender systems are programs that suggest things to users. They learn what users like and dislike. They can also learn what users buy. They use this data to find new things users may want. Many streaming companies use recommender systems to suggest new shows and movies to users.

Companies are using neural networks to predict traffic. Google Maps uses this technology. It learns how traffic moves through an area. This helps it tell how long it will take users to get to their destination.

Weather prediction is another use of neural networks. GraphCast is a weather forecasting model developed in 2023. It was considered to be the most accurate 10-day forecasting software at the time. It could predict extreme weather further into the future than any other system. It was also much faster than other models.

In the future, neural networks may solve even more problems. Experts are still making new kinds of neural networks. And medical researchers are still studying how neurons work. As experts make progress in both fields, the science of neural networks will continue to advance.

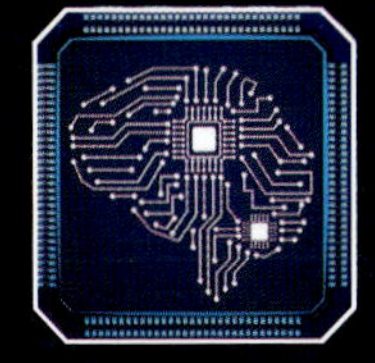

NATURAL LANGUAGE PROCESSING

Natural language processing (NLP) is a field of AI. NLP allows computers to recognize, understand, and create text and speech. In 2001, the first NLP algorithm using neural networks was created. In 2011, Apple developed Siri, the first AI assistant that used neural networks and NLP to understand speech. People could ask Siri to make phone calls. Siri could also search for information on the internet. She would read the information out loud for the user.

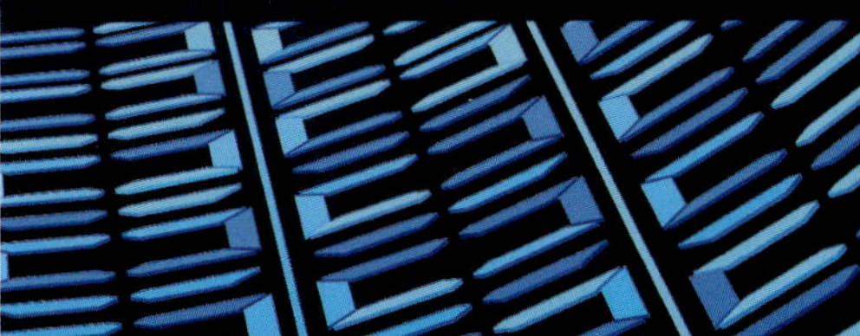

GLOSSARY

chatbot (CHAT-baht) A chatbot is a computer program that can hold humanlike conversations. ChatGPT is an example of a chatbot.

chemical (KEM-ih-kul) Something is chemical if it relates to matter, or physical substances. Neurons in the brain work using chemical signals.

data (DAY-tuh) Data is information collected for a purpose. Neural networks take in data as inputs.

electrical (ee-LEK-trih-kul) Something is electrical if it relates to electricity. Computers are electrical devices.

practical (PRAK-tih-kul) Something practical can be put to use. Practical neural networks can be used to solve real-world problems.

process (PRAH-sess) To process something is to perform a series of actions on it that lead to a result. Neural networks process data in order to produce outputs.

processors (PRAH-seh-surz) Processors are parts of computers that process information. New processors are able to work faster than old ones.

program (PRO-gram) A program is a set of instructions that tells a computer what to do. Neural networks are a kind of program.

psychologist (sy-KAHL-uh-jihst) A psychologist is a person who studies the human mind and human behavior. Psychologist Frank Rosenblatt contributed to the science of neural networks.

structure (STRUK-chur) A structure is an arrangement of parts that form a larger whole. The brain is a structure made of neurons.

FAST FACTS

- A neural network is a type of program inspired by the way the human brain works.
- Neural networks take in data as inputs and produce data as outputs.
- Neural networks can process a very large amount of data.
- A neural network is made of nodes called perceptrons that are modeled after the neurons in a human brain.
- Frank Rosenblatt built the Mark I Perceptron in 1958.
- Deep-learning networks have three or more layers of perceptrons.
- Neural networks are used for predicting the weather, recognizing images and text, recommending things, and predicting traffic.

ONE STRIDE FURTHER

- What are some similarities and differences between a neuron in a brain and a node in a neural network?
- What would happen to a neural network's outputs if it were trained on inaccurate data?
- Think about the problems you need to solve in your everyday life. Could a neural network help you solve any of those problems?

FIND OUT MORE

IN THE LIBRARY

Kelly, Christa. *Benefits of Artificial Intelligence.* Parker, CO: The Child's World, 2025.

Kulz, George Anthony. *What Is Artificial Intelligence?* Parker, CO: The Child's World, 2025.

Rathburn, Betsy. *Artificial Intelligence.* Minneapolis, MN: Bellwether Media, 2021.

ON THE WEB

Visit our website for links about neural networks:
childsworld.com/links

Note to Parents, Caregivers, Teachers, and Librarians: We routinely verify our web links to make sure they are safe and active sites. So encourage your readers to check them out!

INDEX